Understand Bonds & Gilts in a Day

New Edition

Ian Bruce

GLOBAL
professional
publishing

Global Professional Publishing Limited Ltd
Random Acres
Slip Mill Lane
Hawkhurst
Cranbrook
Kent TN18 5AD
http: www.gppbooks.com

© Global Professional Publishing 2009
New Edition 2009

The moral right of the author has been asserted.

ISBN: 978-1-906403-10-2

Printed by Replika Press, India

You should take independent financial advice before acting on material contained in this book.

For full details of Global Professional Publishing titles in Finance, Banking and Management see our website at:
www.gppbooks.com

Contents

ACKNOWLEDGEMENTS

I would like to dedicate this newly revised third edition of Understand Bonds & Gilts In A Day to my wife Pauline and to my children Hannah and Zachary.

My thanks to Chris Brown for his support in writing the original edition of this book, and to Global Professional Publishing for publishing this new edition.

Ian Bruce, 2009

ABOUT THE AUTHOR

Ian Bruce is a successful businessman and the author of more than a dozen books on finance, entrepreneurship and personal development, all of which enjoy a wide international audience. Best known for his ability to present complex ideas in a simple and down to earth manner, he currently resides in mid Wales.

Preface

BONDS AND GILTS are two very similar types of investment which are used by companies and the government respectively to raise capital.

Understand Bonds and Gilts in a Day explains, in simple terms, exactly how bonds and gilts work, why they are used, and how an investor can use them to generate profits as safely as possible.

The aim of this book is not necessarily to encourage investment in bonds and gilts, but simply to give you a detailed overview of the subject in a simple, down to earth context. Once you have this information and are in a position of understanding, you can then make a considered decision as to whether bonds and gilts will suit your own investment needs. If they are, then you will also know how to use them to their best effect.

In the hype-ridden world of the modern age, it is essential that your knowledge of bonds and gilts comes from an unbiased source and not from some slick financial salesman whose prime concern is solely to get your investment business. *Understand Bonds and Gilts in a Day* will tell you about the potential risks as well as the rewards. It will outline the pitfalls as well as the possibilities.

To begin with, each major type of bond and gilt is clearly defined and explained, giving you a solid foundation of knowledge. From there you will learn how to invest in bonds and gilts, calculate the yield and build a well-balanced investment portfolio.

Even the more experienced investor will benefit from this book, thanks to a selection of simple investment strategies which are fully explained and supported by working examples to aid complete understanding.

As if all of that isn't enough, this third edition includes a completely updated chapter on the role that technology plays in the life of investors. Technology has evolved at an incredible rate since the first edition of this book, so you will learn how anyone with an interest in bonds and gilts can take maximum advantage of the computer, mobile and web-based applications that are now available to the individual investor.

In the world of investment, knowledge really is power. The information which follows will allow you to make informed decisions based on cold, hard facts. It will enable you to take positive control over your investment portfolio - however large or small - and subsequently increase the chances of bonds and gilts adding to your personal wealth over the long term.

Introduction

WHEN A PERSON invests in stocks and shares, he effectively buys a portion of the equity in a given company. If the company does well, the shareholder receives a proportion of the profits in the form of a company dividend. The share price might also rise, generating further profits for the investor. If the company does not perform so well, dividends will be lower and the share price might fall, making the overall investment less valuable.

Bonds and gilts are different in that the investor is not purchasing any equity whatsoever. Instead, when an investor purchases bonds he is effectively lending money to a company so that it can pay for a new plant, expand the manufacturing operation or fund some other similar project. In the same way, when an investor purchases gilts he is lending money to the British government so that it can pay for the building of new roads, schools, public utilities and even cover a part of the National Debt. In return for making this loan to either a company or the government, the investor receives a fixed rate of return for a specified length of time, and his original capital (also referred to as "the principal") is repaid in full at the end of the term.

Like all investment tools, bonds and gilts have both positive and negative factors which need to be considered. These are:

Advantages of Bonds and Gilts

◆   The amount of interest an investor will receive is known at the outset. This enables him to accurately project his expected bond and gilt income many years into the future. It also allows him to create a balanced portfolio for a specific purpose, such as retirement or the purchase of a home.

◆ Purchasing bonds and gilts is a very simple process which normally involves little more than contacting a suitable broker by telephone or via the internet.

◆ If interest rates fall then gilts will tend to rise in value.

◆ Bonds and gilts almost always offer better rates of return than can be had by investing in high street deposit accounts.

◆ They are normally less risky than dealing in volatile stocks and shares.

Disadvantages of Bonds & Gilts

◆ If a bond issuer finds that it cannot meet its financial obligations, it may default. This means that it may only repay part of the loan which the investor made when he purchased the bond. In some cases the investor may not receive any repayment at all.

◆ If you tie up your money in bonds and gilts and later find that interest rates rise substantially, your capital may not be available to take advantage of the situation. This means that you may well be "locked in" to an investment which offers less potential profit than you could get elsewhere.

◆ If interest rates rise then gilts will tend to fall in value.

◆ Bonds and gilts do not have the potential of massive gains, as stocks and shares do.

Bonds and gilts are not speculative tools. There is no chance of any investor using them in order to "get rich quick".

They are medium term, medium reward investments, and therefore most suitable for people who want more money than they can get from a deposit account, but who aren't prepared to take the kind of risks involved in the stock market.

Three Steps to Success

Successful investment in bonds and gilts requires the investor to take three fundamental steps. These are:

STEP #1 – Know the Products

There is not just one type of bond and one type of gilt - there are several of each. All have their own characteristics and the first step to success is for the investor to study the pros and cons of each in turn. Only when this has been done can he decide which type of bond or gilt best suits his investment needs.

STEP #2 - Know the Outcome

Before investing it is vital that the various elements of risk, reward and yield have been accurately calculated. This will give the investor a true picture of the most probable outcome, and he can decide on that basis whether or not to proceed with the investment.

STEP #3 - Adopt a Strategy

Whilst it is certainly possible to generate a profit by selecting a single bond or gilt and making a simple investment, most professionals try to increase their chances of long term success by creating a balanced portfolio of investments and then implementing a variety of advanced investment strategies.

Over the course of this book we will look at all of these factors in detail. Beginning with the very basics and proceeding, step-by-step, to the advanced investment techniques used by practising professionals, by the time you turn the last page you will know once and for all how rewarding the world of bonds and gilts can be.

Chapter One

Bonds

DEFINITION: A bond is a promise from a company to pay a lender of money a fixed sum of interest on a regular basis for a stated period. At the end of this period the original loan, or principal, is repaid.

W HEN ANYONE buys a bond, he or she is lending money to a company. The company in question uses the money it raises through bonds to finance expansion projects such as the building of new manufacturing facilities. In return for this loan, the company makes a number of promises to the investor, namely:

◆　　That a fixed amount of interest will be paid to the investor at regular intervals for the life-time of the bond.

◆　　That the original principal will be returned to the investor on a certain maturity date.

Bonds come in a variety of shapes and sizes, but all can be classified as being either short-term, medium-term or long-term.

◆　　Short-term bonds or "Shorts" carry a **maturity date** of up to five years.

♦   Medium-term bonds or "Mediums" carry a maturity date of between five and fifteen years.

♦   Long-term bonds or "Longs" carry a maturity date of more than fifteen years.

The amount of interest which an investor will receive on his bond each year is known as the **nominal** or **coupon yield**. If a bond's **face value** (sometimes called the "**par value**") is £100 and the coupon yield is 6% then the investor can expect to receive a payment of £6 every year until the date of maturity. On the date of maturity the bond will then be redeemed for its face value – so a £100 bond would be redeemed for £100.

During the lifetime of a bond, the market demand for it may rise or fall, and this affects what is known as the **current market value.**

For example, a bond may have been issued to mature in ten years time and give a coupon yield of 6%. If interest rates fall,

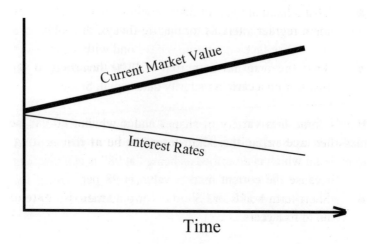

Time

demand for this bond – which offers fixed interest payments of 6% – might increase, and its current market value will rise.

If, on the other hand, interest rates increase, the 6% coupon yield may not be so desirable. Demand for this bond might therefore decline and the current market value will subsequently fall.

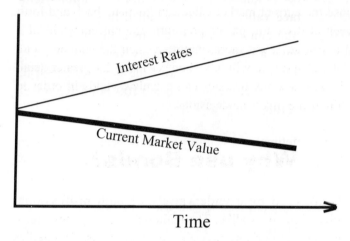

Time

The current market value of a bond is always described as a percentage of the face or par value. If a bond with a face value of £100 has a current market value of £100 then the bond is said to be **at par**, because both values are equal. Similarly:

◆ If a bond has a current market value which is less than the face value, the bond is said to be **at discount**. A bond which is described as being "at 98" is at a discount because the current market value is 98 per cent of the face value. A £100 bond "at 98" would therefore have a current market value of £98.

◆ If a bond has a current market value which is greater than the face value, the bond is said to be **at premium**. A bond which is described as being "at 102" is at a premium because the current market value is 102 per cent of the face value. A £100 bond "at 102" would therefore have a current market value of £102.

Because the current market value can fluctuate back and forth between at discount, par or premium, the current yield of a bond is just as, if not more, important than the coupon yield. In a later chapter we will talk about yields in far greater detail and discuss how the investor can calculate yields in order to help him make investing decisions.

Why use Bonds?

Bonds are used by a wide variety of both professional and private investors alike. The main reasons why they are so popular with the private investing population can be cited as follows:

◆ Bonds offer a fixed income, allowing the investor to control and plan his portfolio years in advance. This is something which just isn't possible with stocks and shares.

◆ Many bonds offer **high liquidity**. This means that the investor can get in or out of a bond investment and does not have to tie his money up for long periods of time unless he wants to.

◆ Bond-holders take priority over share-holders. Should the issuer be unable to meet all of his financial obligations, a bond-holder takes precedence over a share-holder when it comes to being paid. This is because the bond is a debt as far as the issuer is concerned, and debts must be paid before all else.

◆ Trading expenses are minimal. An investor who buys and sells bonds will have to pay a certain amount of commission to his broker, but this sum is minimal when compared with those charged for many other types of investment.

What kind of Bonds are there?

There are many kinds of bonds available, but most can be grouped into one of the following categories:

> Corporate Bonds
> Convertible Bonds
> Euro-Bonds
> Guaranteed Income Bonds
> Junk Bonds
> Zero Bonds

Let us look at each of these in turn and note their key features...

Corporate Bonds

Also known as loan stocks, corporate bonds are issued by companies in order to raise extra capital. They are traded on the stock market but often outperform shares as far as coupon yield (annual interest) is concerned simply because the coupon yield – being fixed – is more reliable than share dividends which rise and fall according to market forces.

If a corporate bond is denominated in and redeemed for sterling then it is – under current legislation – exempt from Capital Gains Tax unless you are investing several hundred thousand pounds. This means that no tax is charged on the profits which such a bond generates for the investor.

What an investor must always bear in mind is that a bond is only as secure as the company behind it. Investors who view security as a major concern may therefore prefer to invest in gilts, which are backed by the government, but more of those later.

A corporate bond can be either "**secured**" or "**unsecured**".

A secured corporate bond is backed by specific company assets (such as plant or machinery) and therefore tends to be a fairly safe investment.

An unsecured corporate bond is not backed by specific company assets, and although a company will always do its best to meet its obligations to unsecured bond-holders, it does not have any specific assets set aside to help meet these obligations. An unsecured bond is therefore only as safe as the company which issues it.

If you want a fixed amount of interest and are confident that the company you are looking at is strong and successful, you might opt to purchase an unsecured corporate bond. But if you want to ensure that there are assets which can – in a worst case scenario – be sold off to return your capital then you should purchase a secured corporate bond instead.

Convertible Bonds

A convertible loan stock (sometimes collectively referred to as "convertibles") is much the same as a corporate bond. The main difference is that a convertible bond gives the investors the right (but not the obligation) to convert their bond(s) into company shares. Whether this option is taken by the investor will depend on the company in question and on the **conversion premium**. This is the price which an investor pays to convert from bonds to ordinary company shares, and when the conversion premium is high the benefits of conversion can be reduced or eroded altogether.

Investors should note that the current market value of a convertible loan stock usually moves up or down in line with the ordinary share price of the company. This means that an investor who purchases a convertible after a rally in share price will probably do so at a premium, and if the share price then falls back overall yield will be decreased.

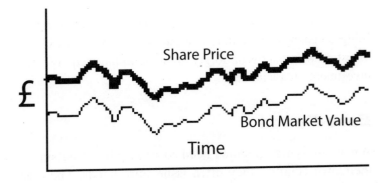

The previous illustration shows how the current market value of a convertible loan stock tends to move up or down roughly in line with the ordinary share price over an extended period.

Consider the following scenario: A company issues a convertible bond with a par value of £100. Share prices then rally and increase by around 30%. In this situation the current market value of the convertible might also increase by 30%. An investor might therefore pay £130 for the convertible bond. Share prices could then fall back to their original levels and remain there until the bond matures. Now the best the investor can hope for is the £100 par value, and may face a discount due to loss of faith in the underlying security.

Because of the way in which convertibles tend to track the ordinary share price, investors would be wise to buy them only when they are at par or at discount.

One final thing you should note about convertibles is the fact that they **almost always offer less interest than a normal corporate bond** simply because they do offer the added conversion option.

Because they can be converted to ordinary shares in the issuing company, convertible loan stocks are most suitable for investors who may want to get involved in more equity based investments at a later date.

Euro-Bonds

When foreign companies need to raise capital outside of their own country, they often issue Euro-bonds. These are sometimes used by investors who believe that sterling will fall against other currencies. But currency fluctuations are generally very difficult to predict and so the majority of private investors tend to give them a wide berth.

It is important to note that profits generated by Euro-bonds are not exempt from Capital Gains Tax unless they are both denominated and redeemed in sterling.

If an investor has an exceptional knowledge of the financial world and has good grounds for believing that the value of sterling will fall in the near future, he may use Euro-bonds to help turn that conviction into a capital gain.

Guaranteed Income Bonds

These are fixed rate bonds which are usually issued by insurance companies and cannot be traded during their lifetimes. This effectively ties the investor down for the lifetime of the bond and once he has made his investment he has little option but to hold it until maturity, which can be anywhere from a year to a decade hence.

If interest rates are likely to fall then Guaranteed Income Bonds can help the investor to lock himself into a fixed (and hopefully higher) rate for a definite term. The downside is that if interest rates rise the investor will not be free to put his money into a more profitable investment vehicle.

The interest generated by a Guaranteed Income Bond can usually be paid to the investor at intervals of between one month and one year, at the discretion of the investor.

Junk Bonds

Junk bonds are very high risk investments. They are usually issued on behalf of companies which have a poor or very low credit rating. In order to attract investors they offer a higher rate but of course the rate of default or non-payment is also higher.

Because of the substantial risks involved in dealing with Junk bonds, this is a market which is generally best avoided by private investors and left to those who are of a far more speculative nature.

Zero Bonds

These bonds do not pay interest and as such have no nominal or coupon yields. For this reason they are sometimes referred to as "Zero-Coupon Bonds". They are issued at a deep discount from the redemption value and so appreciate gradually as the bonds reach their specified maturity dates. At this point the investor receives the face value of the bond and realises his profit.

The following Zero Bond appreciation illustration shows the gradual rise in current market value from its issue at deep discount to its maturity at par value.

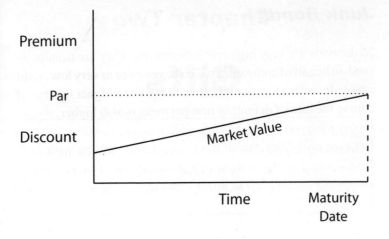

Summary

✔ A bond is a promise from a company to pay a lender of money a fixed sum of interest on a regular basis for a stated period. At the end of this period the original loan, or principal, is repaid.

✔ Bonds offer investors high liquidity and a fixed income.

✔ Trading expenses for bond investors are minimal.

✔ Bond-holders take precedence over share-holders because bonds are debts as far as the issuer is concerned.

✔ A bond is generally only as secure as the company which issues it.

Chapter Two

Gilts

> DEFINITION: A gilt is a promise from the British government to pay a lender of money a fixed sum of interest on a regular basis for a stated period. At the end of this period the original loan, or principal, is repaid.

GILTS OR GILT-EDGED bonds are similar to the bonds which we have already discussed. They are IOU's from an organisation (in this case the British government) promising regular fixed interest payments and repayment of capital on a given maturity date. They are so called because they were originally printed on gilt-edged paper.

Why Does The Government Issue Gilts?

The government offers gilts as a way of paying for the National Debt of the country. The money invested in gilts goes towards projects which should improve the productivity of the country, such as new schools, roads and public utilities. The idea is that as the country becomes more productive, the National Debt will decrease and this will result in greater prosperity for all.

◆ If the size of the National Debt increases, a greater number of gilts are issued to help meet this increase.

Since more gilts become available there is a fall in market demand and gilt prices will fall.

◆ If the government generates a surplus of funds then fewer gilts need to be issued, market demand increases and gilt prices rise.

The titles of gilts generally gives investors quite a lot of information, including the cash payment that the investor can expect each year (the coupon yield) and the year in which the gilt will mature. For example, a "4% Treasury Gilt 2016" is a gilt with a coupon yield of 4% that matures in the year 2016.

Many of the terms applied to bonds also apply to gilts. Gilts have nominal or coupon yields, maturity dates and face or par values. Gilts are also said to be short-, medium- or long-term according to the length of time they have to reach maturity.

Why use Gilts?

Investors use gilts for much the same reasons as they use bonds. Gilts offer a fixed income, high liquidity and do not involve much in the way of trading expenses since they can be bought and sold by post or through a stockbroker. In addition...

◆ All gilts are free from Capital Gains Tax unless you are a very large investor. (You should check the current investment limit for Capital Gains Tax exemption since this changes regularly.)

◆ Because they are backed by the government itself, gilts are safer than bonds. This makes them popular with investors who want security above all, even though yields are often lower than those offered by bonds.

♦ Like most bonds, gilts can be traded during their life-times and their prices rise or fall according to the under-lying interest rates. If interest rates rise then gilt prices will fall, and vice versa. Gilts are therefore excellent in-vestment tools if interest rates are expected to go below their current level.

What kind of Gilts are there?

Like bonds, gilts come in a myriad of varieties, but most fall into one the following categories:

Dated Gilts
Undated Gilts
Index-Linked Gilts
Local Authority Bonds

Dated Gilts

As their name suggests, these are gilts which have a stated ma-turity date. The investor receives fixed levels of interest for the lifetime of the gilt and then redeems it at the end of the term for the face value.

Some gilts have more than one redemption date, and it is up to the government to decide which one will be used. A "7 ¾% Treasury Stock 2012-2015" might therefore be redeemed in any one of four years from 2012 to 2015, at the discretion of the government. The decision about when the gilt will be redeemed will be based on where the government thinks that interests rates are heading.

For example, if interest rates in 2012 were 6% then the coupon yield on our "7 ¾% Treasury Stock 2012-2015" would be 1 ¾% higher. In this case the government would probably want to redeem the gilts as soon as possible so that it could avoid paying the excess. If, on the other hand, interest rates were 8%, the government might let the gilts continue because investors would be receiving slightly less than the prevailing interest rate.

Dated gilts are most useful to investors who want their investment to be as secure as possible and at the same time promise repayment of the principle on a certain date.

Undated Gilts

These are gilts which do not have any redemption date – they simply pay a fixed level of interest year after year. This makes undated gilts prone to excessive erosion from inflation, and thus less popular with most investors.

For example, if you had invested £100 ten years ago in an undated gilt with a coupon yield of 4%, you would receive £4 per year on an ongoing basis. The fact that £4 ten years ago had a great deal more purchasing power than it does today illustrates how inflation effectively reduces the profits of an undated gilt in real terms.

War loans are an example of undated gilts. These were first issued decades ago but inflation has eroded them quite dramatically. Needless to say, investors who still hold war loans are not usually very happy with their performance and would probably avoid undated gilts of all types as a result.

Index-Linked Gilts

Index-linked gilts are dated gilts which are designed to guard against erosion caused by inflation. They are tied to inflation through the **Retail Price Index**. As inflation rises, so does the yield on the gilt. Redemption values are typically lower than with standard dated gilts because of this in-built protection from inflation, but the investor can relax in the knowledge that the purchasing power of his money will not be eaten away over an extended period of time.

If an index-linked gilt carries a coupon yield of 1% then the investor will receive 1% interest plus any rise in the Retail Price Index on a regular basis. Even if inflation soars, the index-linked gilt will ensure that the investor is kept 1% ahead.

This is how an index-linked gilt might perform if inflation rises then levels out:

Index-linked gilts are most suitable for investors who want to secure a fixed amount of interest and at the same time ensure that this interest has the same purchasing power regardless of what happens to inflation.

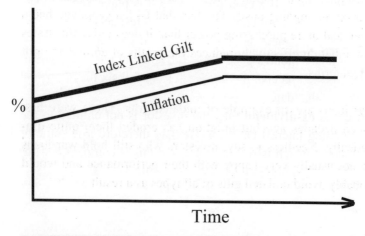

Local Authority Bonds

Also known as **Yearlings**, these are normally issued for just one or two years and are backed by the local authority in question. They generally tend to offer slightly higher returns than regular gilts of a comparable nature, but could be viewed as being a little more risky because they are not issued by the Treasury itself (and so cannot be strictly classified as being gilts).

Local authority bonds are issued so that finance can be raised for projects which are specific to the surrounding geographical area. Many investors purchase local authority bonds simply because they like the idea of giving financial support to a specific part of the country with which they have some emotional association. Others, of course, purchase local authority bonds with their eyes firmly on the yields, sacrificing a little in the way of security for a more profitable return.

Interest Payment Dates

Gilts earn interest on a daily basis, but this interest is only paid twice each year. If a **cum-dividend** gilt is purchased then the investor will be entitled to receive all interest accrued from the last interest payment date. For example, if you buy a cum-dividend gilt two months prior to the next official interest payment date, you will receive the interest for the full six month period preceding that date.

If a gilt is **ex-dividend** then the investor is not entitled to the forthcoming interest payment. He may therefore lose some of the interest which is rightfully his and this is compensated for through a reduction in the price of the gilt.

For example, if you buy an ex-dividend gilt two months prior to the next official interest date you will not receive any interest on that date, and so you will lose out on two months of interest. To reflect this the price you pay for the ex-dividend gilt will be lower.

Just to confuse matters, there are some bonds which will pay interest on a pro-rata basis when sold.

Summary

✔   A gilt is a promise from the British government to pay a lender of money a fixed sum of interest on a regular basis for a stated period. At the end of this period the original loan, or principal, is repaid.

✔   Gilts are issued by the government to help cover part of the National Debt and to fund the building of schools, roads and other public utilities.

✔   Gilts are safer than company-issued bonds because they are backed by the government itself. The price for this added safety, however, is almost always a lower rate of return.

Chapter Three

The Risks and Rewards

A S WITH ALL types of investments, bonds and gilts carry risks as well as rewards. Understanding the nature of the potential down-side in addition to the potential up-side will help you to develop a balanced view of the bond and gilt market, and decide whether or not bonds and gilts will help you to achieve your investment goals.

There are six major risks associated with investing in bonds and gilts. These are:

The Risk of Inflation
The Risk of Default
The Risk of Tax
The Risk of Interest Rates
Selection Risk
Market Risk

Within some of these risks lies an opposing reward. Let us take a look at each one in turn and find out how they affect the bond and gilt investor...

The Risk of Inflation

The greater the level of inflation, the less purchasing power your money will have in the future. This is because inflation erodes the value of your money. So £10,000 in today's money might only be worth £7,000 in ten years time. The graph below illustrates how purchasing power decreases even if inflation stays constant.

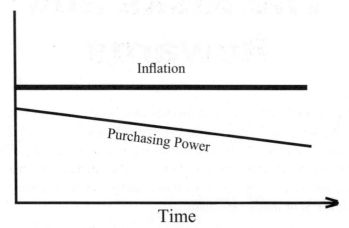

Time

The bond and gilt markets are highly susceptible to the effects of inflation, particularly over the longer term. If you purchase a bond with a coupon yield of 6% and inflation is currently 2.5% then you are effectively making 3.5% (6% minus 2.5% = 3.5%) on your bond after the effects of inflation have been taken into account.

If inflation rises to 5% then your bond will only be generating 1% profit in real terms. Unfortunately, knowing whether inflation will rise substantially in the future is not possible, but collective press opinion is often a good guide.

One way to limit the effects of inflation is to restrict the amount of capital you invest in long term bonds and to review your holdings periodically according to inflation trends. Another is to concentrate on using index-linked investments which are linked to inflation through the Retail Price Index.

Turning our attention in the opposite direction for a moment, inflation can also help an investor to reap rewards. Knowing that a rise in inflation can severely handicap the prices of both bonds and gilts (especially long term ones), a fall in inflation can turbo-boost bond and gilt performance.

For example, if you purchase a bond with a coupon yield of 5% when inflation is at a level of 4% and inflation falls to just 2.5%, you have effectively locked your capital into a position where it earns 2.5% more than inflation (5% – 2.5% = 2.5%). This means that your purchasing power will actually be increased and that is the potential reward as far as inflation is concerned.

The Risk of Default

Everyone who invests in bonds or gilts is lending money – either to a company or to the British Government – and as any bank manager or loan broker will tell you, lending money can be dangerous. By far the biggest danger facing lenders is that of default.

Default occurs when an organisation finds itself in a position where it cannot meet agreed interest or redemption payments and has to delay or even cancel them altogether. Obviously this is not very likely to happen to a gilt which is backed by the government itself, but with company-issued bonds it is a major concern.

For example, a company issues a series of £1,000 bonds with a coupon value of 7% which mature in five years time. The next two years find the company in question battling against heavy competition, and profits fall below the expected projections.

Money becomes tight and the company is left with no choice but to delay interest payments indefinitely.

After keeping its investors waiting for more than a year for outstanding interest payments, the company goes into liquidation. Assets are sold off and the money is used to pay off debts. Unfortunately, debts exceed the realised capital, and so many holders of unsecured bonds will never see their money again.

There are only two ways to reduce the risk of default and these are:

◆ By restricting your investments to large, established companies which have a proven track record of fairly consistent profitability and stability.

◆ By restricting your investments to secured bonds and government-backed gilts.

The Risk of Tax

At the time of writing, both bonds and gilts enjoy a large amount of freedom from the grips of Capital Gains Tax. However, just because tax conditions may currently be favourable towards these investments is no guarantee that they will always be so. Tax legislation can and does change on a regular basis, and so there is a chance that this might go against you at some point in the future.

Some investors might argue that the risk of harsher taxation is too small to worry about, and so far they would have been correct. All risks however – be they large or small – should be given due consideration by the scrupulous investor.

The Risk of Interest Rates

One of the greatest risks is that interest rates will rise, locking the bond or gilt investor into a position where his capital is earning less than it might do elsewhere. In this situation the investor has two possible options:

◆ He can redeem his bond or gilts at a discount. This will almost always generate a capital loss on the investment.

◆ He can hold on until the maturity date and hope that interest rates fall in the meantime. This will mean that the investor may miss out on potential profits which could be made if the money was reinvested in a more productive vehicle.

Whichever option the investor takes, he will lose out. He will either make a capital loss or he will lose indirectly by being forced to miss more lucrative investment opportunities. This, in essence, is the risk of rising interest rates.

The potential reward is for interest rates to fall over the course of a bond or gilt's lifetime. If this happens then – as you have already seen – the investor will be in a position where he is enjoying better than average returns on his capital.

Selection Risk

One risk which many people overlook is known as "Selection Risk". The risk is that when an investor goes about selecting one bond or gilt over another he could very easily make a poor choice. The extent of this risk is directly related to the knowledge and understanding of the investor.

Many private investors (far more than you might think) select their bonds or gilts according to hunches, the tips of financial pundits or by following a more mechanical method which is equally questionable. Yields taken out of context, and big company names, may lull the investor into a false sense of security. A lack of understanding may lead the investor to "stick with what he knows" even though this may not be the wisest choice.

Selection risk can be dramatically reduced if the investor spends some time studying the subject of bonds and gilts thoroughly. If the investor does not have the time or inclination to do this then he may be better off leaving the market alone altogether.

Of course, the potential reward here is that the more an investor learns about the bond and gilt markets, the more successful he is likely to be over the medium to long term.

Market Risk

Because most bonds and gilts are traded openly during their lifetimes, they expose themselves to something called "market risk". This is the volatility of the market itself, and does not necessarily have anything to do with actual changes in inflation or interest rates. Often just the fear or expectation of changes can affect the price of an investment.

For example, you know that bond and gilt prices tend to fall when interest rates increase, but if the market merely fears or expects a rise in interest rates then these prices may fall anyway. Usually, if the expectation is unfounded then the bonds and gilts will climb back to their proper position, but this may not happen immediately.

There is little anyone can do about guarding against market risk except to be aware of it and, perhaps, avoid buying bonds or gilts at a premium. On the flip side, taking advantage of market risk would normally involve purchasing at discount during a fear-induced price fall and then perhaps selling at par or greater when the market recovers.

Evaluating Risks

Knowing what the risks and rewards are will enable you to decide if bonds and gilts suit both your personality and investment needs. The fact is that some people have a very low risk threshold and would find the prospect of rising interest rates causing their investments to fall in value rather frightening.

Other people have higher risk thresholds and would be quite happy to ride along the ups and downs of market volatility if they thought they stood a fair chance of making a good return on maturity.

The thing you must remember is that potential risk is almost always directly linked to potential rewards. If you want to stand a chance of making exceptional gains then you will probably need to take exceptional risks. If you would be happy with very small, limited gains then you would only need to take very small, limited risks.

As a general rule, if the safety of your capital is of prime concern then dated gilts and secured corporate bonds should be chosen over other securities. If you are willing to sacrifice a little in the way of safety in order to gain a potentially higher reward then local authority bonds, unsecured corporate bonds and convertibles might be more appropriate.

You can see the direct relationship between risk and reward quite clearly in the following graph:

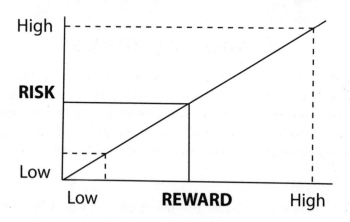

Summary

✔ All forms of investment carry elements of both risk and reward. Bonds and gilts are no exception to this rule.

✔ There are six major types of risk which you should be aware of: risk of inflation, risk of default, risk of tax, risk of interest rates, selection risk and market risk.

✔ Whether you choose to accept a risk or not depends on your own personal circumstances, goals and risk threshold.

✔ Risk and reward are directly related to each other. High risk investments usually offer high potential rewards. Low risk investments usually offer low potential rewards.

Chapter Four

Investing in Bonds & Gilts

BEFORE YOU can accomplish anything in life, you first need to be quite clear about what your objectives are. Unless you know where your destination is, you are very unlikely to catch the right train. The same applies to investing, and unless you know what your goal is, you are very unlikely to select the bonds or gilts which will enable you to achieve it swiftly and with a minimum of fuss.

The objectives of both private and professional investors vary wildly. Some private investors want to obtain a fixed level of income as securely as possible. Others may want to use bonds as a "stepping stone" into the world of stock market investments, and are therefore willing to take on a greater level of risk in return for an increase in potential profits. The bonds or gilts these people choose to invest in will therefore differ according to their needs

Professional investors working on behalf of banks, insurance companies and similar organisations often use bonds and gilts to put excess money to work without a great element of risk. Banks, for example, regularly invest in short term gilts to generate interest on money which has been placed in deposit accounts. In such cases, short term gilts are selected because they usually offer very high levels of liquidity. The money can therefore be accessed quickly if there is a sudden rush of customers withdrawing money from their accounts.

We will look at the subject of private investment goals and how bonds and gilts could help the investor to achieve them in Chapter Six. In the meantime, let us discuss one of the most fundamental keys to success whatever your financial objectives may be...

Introducing
"The Pyramid Principle"

The Pyramid Principle states that the investments of any individual or organisation should be set up in such a way so that there is a balance of risk. There should be three sections to this investment pyramid – a wide foundation of very secure, low yield investments, a smaller mid-section of medium risk, medium reward investments and an even smaller peak of higher risk investments which give the potential for even higher gains. The pyramid would therefore look something like this:

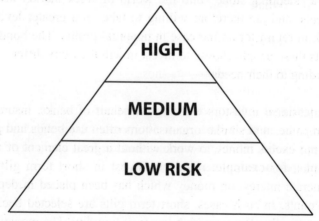

The purpose of The Pyramid Principle is to try and ensure that no investor – either private or corporate – becomes "top heavy" by taking on a lot of high risk investments without first having a solid base and mid-section of low and medium risk investments. Let's look at these three sections of low, medium and high risk in turn and see how they apply to the bond and gilt markets...

Low Risk Base

This is as secure as can be. Most simple deposit accounts offered by banks and building societies fall into this range. These vehicles generally offer only small potential rewards but give the investor a very good element of capital safety. Dated and Index-linked gilts would fall into this category because they are backed by the government and there is little chance of default.

No investor should contemplate taking on medium or high risks until he has first built a dependable low risk base of capital which – although probably not earning a great deal – can be relied on whatever the markets may be doing.

Medium Risk Mid-Section

Medium risk investments are those which offer more potential rewards but still leave most of the capital fairly secure. Individual Savings Accounts (ISA's) and Unit Trusts are generally said to be in this range. So are corporate bonds which are issued by solid, reliable companies that are least likely to default on interest or redemption payments.

The medium risk section of the pyramid is designed to give the investor a higher level of return without taking very big risks.

Again, until you have built this section of your pyramid you shouldn't get involved in the next level, which are high-risk investments.

High Risk Peak

High risk investments include derivatives (such as traded options), individual stocks and shares and bonds of a speculative nature such as Junk Bonds. This high-risk peak should only be built when the earlier sections of your pyramid have been established. Investing in high-risk investments before that point could ruin you financially if things go wrong.

Once you understand The Pyramid Principle you should be able to see immediately which bonds or gilts would best suit your current financial situation. This automatically narrows down the vehicles available to you and helps to guard against the Selection Risk which we spoke about in the last chapter.

How to Deal in Bonds And Gilts

The majority of individual investors buy and sell their bonds and gilts through a stockbroker. Even those investors who do much of the work themselves online will usually do so via the website of a stockbroker, so essentially they are still dealing with a broker, as opposed to dealing directly with the Government (in the case of gilts) or individual companies (for bonds).

It is possible to buy newly issued gilts direct from the Debt Management Office of the Government, and a limited range of products is also available from the Post Office. However, stockbrokers are able to offer a much more complete range of bonds and gilts, and will allow you to buy and sell these as and when you please.

Whilst previous generations of investors were often quite happy to buy bonds and gilts by mail, this method of dealing has all but disappeared. Dealing by telephone or via the internet helps an investor to have more control over the price he deals at, and therefore to buy and sell with more precision.

Selecting a stockbroker

There are two types of brokers available to private investors. These are traditional stockbrokers and execution-only stockbrokers.

A traditional stockbroker will give his client advice, recommendations and market pointers in addition to buying or selling on the client's behalf. This advice can be extremely valuable for investors who are new to bonds and gilts, and will often help them to avoid some of the risks we spoke about in the last chapter.

Because traditional stockbrokers do more than just buy and sell, the commissions they charge tend to be slightly higher than those charged by execution-only brokers, but this additional expense may well be a price worth paying.

An execution-only stockbroker does not give his client any advice, recommendations or market pointers. He simply acts as the middleman between the investor and the market, buying and selling on his clients behalf. Execution only brokers usually offer the lowest commissions but investors must be prepared to make their own decisions and live by the results. If you are fully conversant with financial jargon and understand the field you want to invest in thoroughly then an execution-only broker may well meet your needs, otherwise it would be better to err on the side of caution and deal through a traditional broker who will help you take your first steps into the market.

Selecting either a traditional or execution-only broker is largely a matter of shopping around and finding one which will be most suitable. The main questions you need to ask any broker you are considering are:

What type of new clients is he accepting, if any?

Some brokers will only accept new clients who intend to put substantial amounts of business their way. Others are more than happy to accept small private investors. Discovering at the outset whether the broker you are talking to would be willing to take on your business might save you a great deal in the way of wasted time.

What are your commission rates?

Don't beat around the bush when it comes to talking about money – after all, this is what brokers talk about all day long. Most brokers charge commission according to a sliding scale. This obviously means that the larger your investments are, the more commission you will pay. Almost all brokers establish a minimum commission fee which is payable on all transactions below a certain limit. Ask for both minimum commission details and sliding scale rates and this will help you to compare the broker with the others you contact.

Are there any other charges?

Often you won't need to ask this question because the broker will tell you about any additional fees when discussing commissions. If he doesn't, find out if he charges any management fees over and above the commission rates – most do.

Some brokers who manage their clients portfolios set fees which are related to the performance of the portfolio they control. This motivates them to make the best returns they can, so if you are aiming to have a broker take care of your portfolio and make your decisions for you, a fee which is directly related to performance might be a good thing.

What is your track record?
Some brokers are better than others when it comes to making money grow. Ask about past performance and you will get some idea of how useful his advice is. Obviously, if you are looking for an execution-only broker then you should not ask this question because no advice will be given and so past performance does not exist.

One you have telephoned a few brokers, read through their literature and/or visited their official web sites, a decision can be made on the basis of the information you have accumulated. Ask around your friends and acquaintances and see if you know anyone who has any personal recommendations.

If you do then you can take these recommendations into account before making a final decision. Finally, if you are still unsure about which broker to use, consider consulting a professional financial advisor.

Registering with a Broker

Having found a suitable broker which you would like to deal with, you must then register as one of his clients. Normally this will involve little more than completing a few application forms and sending the broker a cheque (or online payment) which he can then invest according to your instructions.

Sometimes however – especially if you want your broker to make your investment decisions for you – an informal meeting may be suggested so that you can discuss your objectives and investment preferences more fully.

Taking Professional Advice

A professional financial advisor is someone who is used to helping people get their investments in order by analysing their situation and giving specific recommendations.

There are two types of advisors: **Tied Advisors** are tied to one financial company and can therefore only recommend products and services sold by that company.

Independent Financial Advisors are not tied to any one company and can therefore recommend products and services from across the whole spectrum of the financial world. They *should* be unbiased.

If you consult a professional advisor he will be able to help you ensure that your pyramid of investments is evenly (and therefore most effectively) built. He will also be able to tell you about bonds and gilts as well as new issues which are not yet known to most private investors, and suggest which of these would be best suited to your own individual needs.

Tracking your investments

Whether you take total control over your bond and gilt investments or leave the majority of the decision making to a qualified professional, as an astute investor you should know how to track your investments from week to week by interpreting the figures published in national daily newspapers.

Reading and interpreting the data is very simple once you understand how it is laid out. Here is how a gilt might be listed in the "Mediums" section of the financial pages...

Tr   5pc   '25 →   116.1   -0.18   117.79   98.32

First of all, the name of the gilt, the coupon and the maturity date is given. The gilt above is therefore a Treasury with a coupon yield of 5 per cent which matures in the year 2025.

The following figures in turn tell us the current market value (116.10), the change in market value (-0.18), the highest value of this gilt in the past 52 weeks (117.79) and the lowest value in the past 52 weeks (98.32). We can therefore see that the current value of this gilt is not far from the 52 week high, and that the gilt is being sold at a premium.

Most investors use this data so that they know exactly how their money is performing even if a professional is making the majority of their decisions. Others, however, use it to help them deal in a more speculative manner.

The Speculators

Bonds and Gilt speculators are individuals who aim to use the more volatile movements in current market values to help them generate profits. They are generally people who have a very high risk threshold and view the markets as something of an elaborate roulette wheel.

The tactics of speculators differ widely, but one strategy which they commonly use is to purchase more volatile securities at discount and then sell them back to the market when they reach par or premium. The more volatile the security, the faster these deals can be completed to the satisfaction of the speculator.

Speculating with bonds and gilts is not something which the more sedate investor should consider getting involved in unless he is truly prepared to take big risks and probably take some hefty losses which may well outstrip any increased gains.

Summary

✔ Before you can invest wisely, you must know what your aims are. Specific objectives and possible strategies for meeting them will be looked at in a later chapter.

✔ The Pyramid Principle should help any investor to meet their objectives safely. It states that the investments of any individual or organisation should be set up in such a way so that there is a balance of risk.

✔ Bonds and gilts are most often bought and sold through a stockbroker, and transactions with stockbrokers are usually made by telephone or via the internet.

✔ There are two types of brokers – traditional brokers, which give advice, and execution-only brokers which simply buy and sell according to the investor's instructions.

✔ Selecting a broker is a matter of shopping around, asking the right questions and choosing one which meets your personal needs.

✔ Qualified advice can be taken from professional financial advisors. Some are tied to one financial organisation but others are truly independent and can give unbiased advice from across the whole spectrum of the financial world.

✔ Bond and gilt investors can keep track of how their money is performing by learning to interpret the data published on the financial pages of most newspapers.

✔ Some individuals use market data to help them become speculators, but this is a high risk occupation which should not even be considered by most investors.

Chapter Five

Calculating Yield

> *DEFINITION: The amount of money which a bond or gilt will produce for the investor, normally expressed as a percentage.*

Yield is one of the easiest ways of comparing one bond or gilt with another – in principle. In reality, however, yield figures may not tell the whole story.

For example, if a "Treasury 4.25% 2027" gilt was compared with a "Treasury 4.75% 2020" then one might think that the latter would be the better investment option because the nominal yield is greater. Such a conclusion fails to identify that the first gilt has a longer run to maturity, and so may actually offer the investor a better return despite having a lower nominal yield.

Just as there are many ways to compare bonds and gilts, there are several types of yield which can be calculated. These are known as

Nominal (or Coupon) Yield
Current Yield
Yield to Maturity

Nominal or Coupon Yield

As we saw in an earlier chapter, the nominal or coupon yield is how much a bond or gilt will generate each year in the way of interest. It is based on the rate which the issuer has obliged himself to pay on the face or par value of the bond.

For example, a £1,000 bond carrying a coupon yield of 5% will pay the investor £50 each year in interest. This is calculated by multiplying the par value of the bond (or gilt) by the nominal or coupon yield figure, as follows:

$$£1,000 \times 5\% = £50$$

Nominal yield calculations are the easiest of all to perform, but are very limited in their use. They only tell the investor how much he can expect to receive in interest during any single year.

Current Yield

Current yield is how much a bond or gilt is generating in the way of interest based on the current market value, which might be at par, discount or premium.

You might think that any bond or gilt with a coupon yield of ten per cent would give a current yield of ten per cent, but that is not the case. Consider the following:

If you purchased a £100 bond at a premium of 102 and the nominal yield is 5%, you would not receive 5% of your investment as an interest payment. This is because the stated nominal yield of 5% refers to the yield when the bond is at par, not at a discount or premium.

To calculate the true current yield of any bond or gilt, you must divide the normal amount of annual interest by the current market value of the bond in question.

For example, if our £100 bond is still at a premium of 102 (costing us £102) and the nominal yield is 5%, the normal amount of interest this bond would generate would be £5. Our calculation to find the true current yield would therefore be:

$$£5 \text{ divided by } £102 = 0.049$$

We then multiply this resultant figure by one hundred to give us the current yield as a percentage figure:

$$0.049 \times 100 = 4.9\%$$

The actual current yield is therefore one tenth of a percentage point less than the stated nominal yield.

Let us go through another example. Imagine that we purchase a £100 bond with a 5% nominal yield at a discount of 96. The bond therefore costs us £96. The normal amount of annual interest would by £5 (5% of £100 par value). We would calculate the current yield as follows:

$$£5 \text{ divided by } £96 = 0.052$$
$$0.052 \times 100 = 5.2\%$$

Because we purchased this bond at a discount the true current yield is one fifth of a percentage point greater than the stated nominal yield.

As you can see, current yield calculations are of much more use to the investor than straight forward nominal or coupon yield calculations. They enable the investor to find out in real terms exactly how hard his capital is working.

The problem with both nominal and current yield calculations, however, is that they are confined to the present moment or year. They cannot tell the investor how much he can expect to make over the longer term. To gain this knowledge the investor must use a third form of yield calculation...

Yield to Maturity

Also known as the redemption yield calculation, the yield to maturity calculation takes into account the fact that any investor who holds a bond or gilt to the date of maturity will not only receive interest payments but may also make a capital gain or loss on redemption. The calculation therefore gives the investor a figure which represents the true gain on the whole lifetime of his investment.

The yield to maturity calculation is used by professionals and involves a lot of complex mathematics which take compounded interest into account. Having said that, a fairly accurate, *but not exact*, yield to maturity calculation can be done by anyone with a pocket calculator and a few minutes to spare.

To calculate yield to maturity you must:

◆   Take the price you are considering paying for a bond or gilt and divide any premium or discount by the number of years the investment has to run. This generates an average capital gain or loss figure.

◆ Divide this average figure by the price you are thinking about paying for the bond or gilt, then multiply by 100 to generate a percentage capital gain or loss on the investment.

◆ Take this percentage loss or gain and subtract or add it to the nominal or coupon yield accordingly. This generates the final yield to maturity figure.

Let us run through an example to make this perfectly clear. If you are considering purchasing a £1,000 bond with a nominal yield of 5% at a discount of 96, you will pay £960 for the bond. The current yield on this bond would be:

$$£50 \text{ divided by } £960 = 0.052$$
$$0.052 \times 100 = 5.2\%$$

If the bond has ten years to run then the discount you obtained of £40 (£1,000 par value minus the £960 you paid = £40) must be divided by ten:

$$£40 \text{ divided by } 10 \text{ years} = £4$$

This means that you will make an average annual capital gain of £4 on an investment of £960. If we divide the capital gain by the investment and multiply by one hundred we can convert this to a percentage figure:

$$£4 \text{ divided by } £960 = 0.004$$
$$0.004 \times 100 = 0.4\%$$

Add this to the current yield of 5.2% and you will have the final Yield to Maturity figure.

$$0.4\% + 5.2\% = 5.6\%$$

This method of calculating yield to maturity, as mentioned earlier, is not accurate to the nth degree because compounding effects are over simplified. But it does give a good indication of how much you can expect to make over the lifetime of the investment. In the case above you will make around 5.6% on your investment even though the coupon yield is just 5%. This is because the bond is being offered at a discount.

If the bond or gilt were offered at a premium then the yield to maturity value would obviously be less than this. Consider another example:

On offer is a £1,000 bond with a nominal yield of 5% at a premium of 104. You would therefore pay £1,040 for the bond. The current yield on this bond would be:

$$£50 \text{ divided by } £1,040 = 0.048$$
$$0.048 \times 100 = 4.8\%$$

If the bond has ten years to run then the premium you obtained of £40 (£1,040 you paid minus the £1,000 par value = £40) must be divided by ten:

$$£40 \text{ divided by } 10 \text{ years} = £4$$

This means that you will make an average annual capital loss of £4 on your investment of £1,040. If we divide the capital loss by the investment and multiply by one hundred we can convert this to a percentage figure:

$$£4 \text{ divided by } £1,040 = 0.003$$
$$0.003 \times 100 = 0.3\%$$

Deduct this from the current yield of 4.8% and you will have the final Yield to Maturity figure.

$$0.3\% - 0.3\% = 4.5\%$$

This figure indicates that you will make around 4.5% on your investment even though the bond has ten years to run and the coupon yield is 5%. This is because the bond is being offered at a premium.

The yield to maturity calculation is an excellent way for the investor to find out how much money he stands to make or lose over the lifetime of his gilt or bond. The calculation itself may look a little complex but it takes just a few minutes once you are familiar with it. For those who simply cannot bear the thought of crunching numbers, or those who want more exact percentages, professional compiled yield to maturity figures are published daily in the *Financial Times*.

Using Yield Calculations

Although yield calculations can help investors to compare bonds and gilts with each other, selecting investments on yield figures alone is not the wisest approach to take.

Other factors must be considered, such as the reliability and past performance of a bond issuer, whether the investment gives protection against inflation and whether interest rates are likely to rise or fall.

When using yield to maturity figures you must also bear in mind that these indicate what your capital might earn only if you hold your bonds or gilts to the redemption date. They cannot indicate what capital gain or loss you might make if you sell your holdings before that date at the market value, which could be at an altogether different discount or premium.

Summary

✔   The yield of a bond or gilt is the amount of money which it will produce for the investor, normally expressed as a percentage.

✔   The nominal or coupon yield is how much a bond or gilt will generate each year in the way of interest in relation to the face or par value.

✔   ·The current yield is how much a bond or gilt is generating in the way of interest based on the current market value, which might be at par, discount or premium.

✔   The yield to maturity tells the investor how much they can expect to make on an investment as a whole provided they hold it until the redemption date.

✔   Yield calculations are extremely useful in providing the investor with profit forecasts, but should not be used exclusively to make selections. Other factors such as company fundamentals and past performance must also be taken into account.

Chapter Six

Building a Portfolio

DEFINITION: A portfolio is a varied collection of investments which through diversity give a certain element of stability. They are usually built with a specific objective in mind.

Consider the case of Mr Brown. He is a man who wants to use bonds and gilts to help him prepare for retirement in ten years time and has £30,000 to invest in them. He is attracted to corporate bonds because of the good returns they tend to offer, but is a little worried about the greater level of risk they involve. He could opt to invest in more secure gilts, but these don't offer the kind of returns he wants to make.

The best solution to Mr Brown's quandary would be to build a portfolio of various bonds and gilts which would offer him good returns and good security at the same time. He would split his £30,000 into perhaps twenty separate funds of £1,500 and make twenty different investments – some in gilts for security and some in corporate bonds for higher potential gains.

By spreading his total portfolio capital of £30,000 over twenty different investments, our friend will be spreading his risks. If a couple of bonds decrease in value, other may increase and so the loss is counterbalanced. If he had placed all £30,000 into just one bond and it had subsequently decreased in value, the loss would have been far more substantial. Of course this is a highly simplistic view of how a portfolio works, but it does serve to illustrate how they can be used to help spread risks.

A well diversified portfolio can help give your investments a general balance between risk and reward. But diversification can also help to smooth any delays between the interest payments you receive on your individual holdings.

A bond and/or gilt portfolio should be part of a larger financial plan. No one would ever suggest that an investor put all of his money into bonds and gilts. As we said earlier, the astute investor will follow The Pyramid Principle and make sure that they have a solid base of low-risk investments before branching out into other areas.

The bond portfolio itself should also be well balanced and follow the pyramid structure, as illustrated below:

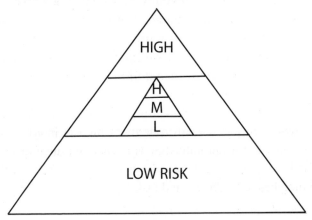

Here you can see that within the larger financial plan of the investor a separate bonds and gilts portfolio (indicated by the smaller pyramid) has been established in the medium-risk section. This pyramid also has three levels so the investor can spread their capital over low to medium, medium and medium to high risk investments.

This visualisation of "a balanced portfolio within a larger financial plan" should help you to see how everything we have discussed so far fits together.

The building of a balanced portfolio can only commence once the investor has decided what his objectives are. Let us take a look at two of the most common financial goals investors have and examine how bonds and gilts might figure in their attainment...

Retirement

Although most people acknowledge that preparing for retirement is something which is vitally important, few begin planning for this event early enough. The fact is that the sooner anyone begins planning their retirement fund, the more time they will have to generate a substantial amount of capital, which will help them enjoy their golden years to the full.

Many people only discover this when it is too late, and find themselves with just a small retirement fund and only ten or twenty years left to go until they are scheduled to stop working. If these people want to truly enjoy their retirement then something has to be done – and fast.

The first thing these people should do is ensure that they are making the maximum pension contributions they are permitted to make. This is because pension contributions are – at the time of writing – deducted from gross income and therefore exempt from income tax.

That done, they can then start building a portfolio which is geared for capital growth. Bonds and gilts (depending on the investor's attitude towards risk) can either be used exclusively or to give a more secure balance to a higher risk portfolio of, for example, stocks and shares.

Bonds and gilts may also be useful when the investor reaches retirement age and collects a lump sum from his pension. The lump sum can be used to build a stable and fairly reliable income-based portfolio which will support his normal pension payments and help to increase the quality of his life.

Long Term Savings

Many people have long term goals for five or more years hence and investors can use bonds and gilts to help prepare for these events in much the same way as they would if they were planning for retirement. The most popular goals over recent years have been:

- ◆ To generate funds for further education expenses for children in ten years time
- ◆ To pay for a child's wedding in five years time
- ◆ To buy a holiday home in twenty years time
- ◆ To take a diamond anniversary cruise in eight years time

Again, to reach these goals (and others like them) a portfolio can be built with growth in mind. Either higher risk investments such as stocks and shares or less risky investments such as corporate bonds can be counterbalanced to a degree with gilt-edged investments. The exact mixture of security and risk is obviously up to the investor and must be based on his own risk tolerance level.

Knowing how much his bonds and gilts stand to generate over their lifetimes (by using the yield to maturity calculation given in an earlier chapter) the investor can review his portfolio at regular intervals and thus ensure that when the money is needed, it is there for the taking.

Inflation and Portfolios

Because inflation can erode any investment which is not index-linked, you should think carefully about making sure that you have an element of equity in your portfolio.

Equity in the form of shares might be suitable for investors who are willing to take greater risks, but even investors with lower risk thresholds can prepare for inflation by adding a few convertible bonds to their portfolios. These will give the investor the opportunity of converting these bonds into ordinary shares, the prices of which will tend to rise roughly in line with inflation.

Index-linked bonds can of course be used to help protect your capital from the ravages of inflation, but remember that these will probably offer lower returns than other bonds and gilts because of their unique nature.

The Flexibility of a Portfolio

What all investors must remember is that a portfolio should not be seen as a rigid collection of fixed investments which is to be built and then left alone. Rather, it should be viewed as a highly flexible organism which can be adapted to suit changing economic situations and developments as and when they occur.

If you are not prepared to take such a "hands on" approach to your portfolio then you may be better off letting a professional manage your portfolio, or considering one of the alternative options which have become increasingly popular over recent years...

Unit Trusts

A Unit Trust is an investment vehicle in which money from a group of investors is pooled and used to create a diverse portfolio on their behalf. Each investor is allocated a number of units according to the size of his original investment and will receive the relevant proportion of profits after all costs and charges have been taken into consideration.

To illustrate how a unit trust works, consider this example: A company invests £3 Million in a wide variety of stocks and securities. It splits this portfolio into 1,000 separate units. Each unit therefore costs £3,000.

The portfolio does well and the £3 Million grows to some £5 Million. Each unit is now worth £5,000 (£5m divided by 1,000 units = £5,000) and so any investor who bought a unit at the original price of £3,000 will have made £2,000 profit before charges. What is more, the individual investors leave all investment decisions and portfolio management to the unit trust company.

Individual investors can leave unit trusts at any time by selling their units, but they should primarily be seen as medium to long term investments. Similarly, they can increase their holdings by purchasing further units whenever they want. The cost of units, however, will obviously rise and fall according to the performance of the trust itself.

Many Unit Trusts are geared primarily for growth and tend to concentrate on equity based investments such as stocks and shares. A growing number, however, are geared towards income generation, and it is in these that a prospective bond or gilt investor will have most interest.

A UK Gilt and Fixed Interest Unit Trust, for example, is one which invests a minimum of 80% of its total fund in British gilts and other fixed-income securities. What the remaining 20% of the fund is invested in is up to the trust managers, but commonly it is placed in higher risk stocks and shares to give the fund a general guard against inflation.

The main advantages of investing in Unit Trusts are:

◆ An individual investor can spread his money over a much wider range of securities in a unit trust than would be possible if he built his own portfolio. This is because the unit trust is a pool of money, and something like £3 Million from 1,000 separate investors can be spread more thinly than a much smaller individual fund of £3,000.

◆ Unit Trusts are handled by professional fund managers, so the individual investors do not have to make any specific portfolio management decisions.

Before deciding to get involved with any particular unit trust – be it geared for growth or income – you must bear in mind that different unit trusts will have different performance records. Some unit trusts have done extremely well in the past whilst others have not. Of course, past performance cannot be taken as a guarantee of what might happen in the future, but it makes sense that you should look to join a winning team if you decide to join one at all.

ISAs

Individual Savings Accounts (or **ISAs**) are savings and investment vehicles that are extremely tax efficient because any interest earned or capital gains that are made are deemed tax-free as far as the UK taxation system is concerned. Of course, there are limits on how much can be saved or invested in an ISA, and these are revised on an annual basis. The tax efficiency of ISAs may also change if the Government chooses to amend the rules that govern them in the future.

At the time of writing there are two types of ISA, and these are known as the Cash ISA and the Stocks & Shares ISA. The Cash ISA is designed for individuals who simply want to save their money (up to a maximum limit) without paying any tax on the interest earned on those savings. The Stocks & Shares ISA allows investors to invest directly or indirectly in stocks and shares (again, up to a maximum limit) and enjoy freedom from tax on dividend payments as well as Capital Gains Tax.

An investor may have a Cash ISA, a Stocks & Shares ISA, or both. The maximum investment allowed in each will depend on which ISA is used and if both are used. Generally speaking, whatever amount of money you save in a Cash ISA automatically reduces the maximum amount that can be invested in a Stocks & Shares ISA. The only way to invest the maximum in a Stocks & Shares ISA is therefore to not have a Cash ISA.

It cannot be stressed enough that the tax-free nature of ISAs is not something that can be counted on for the long term. Not only can the tax rules be changed (to make ISAs more or less tax efficient, depending on the mood of a particular budget) but ISAs themselves could be replaced by an alternative vehicle in the future, just as ISAs themselves were launched in 1999 to effectively replace Personal Equity Plans (PEPs). Almost all investors should therefore take full advantage of ISAs whilst they can, but they should not adopt the belief that the rules governing ISAs will always remain the same, because they won't.

ISAs are available from a wide variety of professional fund managers, and it is always worth shopping around for the plan which is most suited to your needs. For the bond investor in particular, Corporate Bond ISAs may be worth looking into, but these will obviously under-perform equity-based ISAs. And of course, if an investor pays little or no tax he should decide if the management charges for ISAs are worth paying, since he will not benefit a great deal from the tax breaks which the plans offer.

For other investors who would normally pay a fair amount of tax on their investments and have not already taken advantage of the facility, ISAs may well be a godsend. They do however (like any investment plan) have to be thought about carefully before any firm investment decision is made.

Building a portfolio or investing in one which is built and managed on your behalf can help to spread the risks and rewards of a variety of stocks and/or securities. They can be geared primarily towards growth or income and investors can therefore use them to help attain their financial goals, whatever they may be.

Summary

✔ A portfolio is a varied collection of investments which through diversity give a certain element of stability. They are usually built with a specific objective in mind.

✔ A well diversified portfolio can help to give your investments a general balance between risk and reward.

✔ Portfolios should be well balanced and follow the pyramid structure, mixing low, medium and higher risk investments.

✔ A Unit Trust is an investment vehicle in which money from a group of investors is pooled and used to create a diverse portfolio on their behalf.

✔ Individual Savings Accounts (ISAs) allow you to save and invest a certain amount of money in a more tax-efficient way than you would be able to enjoy otherwise. You can save in a Cash ISA, invest in a Stocks & Shares ISA, or both, and financial advice is always worth taking before you make any final decision.

Chapter Seven

Bond Investment Strategies

Contrary to popular belief, professional fund managers are not miracle workers. They cannot predict what will happen in the future any more than anyone else can. The reason a professional fund manager often succeeds in generating substantial long term profits when so many others fail is because he uses a selection of advanced investment strategies to help him make his investment decisions.

There is little room in a book of this nature to discuss the sometimes extremely complex investment strategies which professional fund managers use. However, there is room to introduce a handful of slightly more advanced strategies which will help the reader to invest with substantially more confidence and – hopefully – generate a greater overall return on his capital.

The strategies we will discuss in this chapter are simply more involved courses of action which are designed to help the investor to either increase profits or minimise losses. They are not – as I have said – complex actions, but they will demand that the investor commits some time and effort to his portfolio and take a more "hands on" approach.

The eight investment strategies which are discussed on the following pages can be used by all bond and gilt investors, be they novices or more experienced. They can be used individually or – for total investment control – on a collective basis, and many are supported by examples of how they work in action.

Strategy #1
Give Yourself a Financial Review

It has been said that most people spend more time planning their annual holidays than they do their finances. One of the keys to investment success in bonds and gilts – as in other areas – is to sit down and review your current situation and future goals in a logical manner with a view to developing a solid plan of action.

The first step in giving your a financial review is to take a look at your current financial status. Calculate your total income and then your outgoings. The difference is usually positive, and this signifies the amount of capital which you can afford to invest in different areas.

When you know how much capital you have available, you can focus on ensuring that a sum of money is set aside in a highly liquid deposit account for emergencies and that basic financial events have been adequately prepared for, such as the inevitability of death (which is prepared for by taking out life insurance) and retirement.

If these major items have been attended to then the remaining capital can be comfortably invested in bonds, gilts and other vehicles.

Example

Mr Howarth has just been made redundant and has received a lump sum of £19,000. He is getting close to retirement age and wants to put this money into a managed portfolio of bonds and gilts in preparation for this event.

He reviews his financial situation and realises that although he has used up his pension allowance and taken out adequate life cover, he does not have much in the way of emergency savings. He therefore takes £5,000 of his redundancy payment and places it in a secure deposit account. The rest he invests as planned in a managed portfolio.

If Mr Howarth had not given himself a financial review then he might have gone ahead and invested the whole £19,000, only to find that some months later he needed access to some of this so that he could meet some unexpected expenses. This might have made it necessary to sell some of his holdings at the current market value and could, if these were below par, have generated a capital loss.

Performing your own financial review is a strategy which is designed to prevent you from tying up money in bonds and gilts which you later discover you really need access to, and which would therefore be better placed in very short term investment vehicles.

Strategy #2
Don't Give Money Away

One of the things which professional financial advisors discover again and again is that far too many people are unknowingly giving some of their money away simply because they have not made use of all the tax-exempt investment vehicles which are available to them.

For example, bond and gilt investors who are thinking of using securities to prepare for retirement must first ensure that they are contributing as much as they are allowed to a regular personal or company pension scheme.

This will not only help to build retirement funds in a tax-free environment, but will also help to cut their income tax bill, which in turn may leave more money available for their eventual bond and gilt investments.

Example

Mr Jones has just received an inheritance of £10,000. He intends to invest this in a self-managed portfolio of blue chip stocks balanced with more secure corporate bonds and dated gilts. This is so that he can make his retirement as comfortable as possible in ten years time.

After looking at his finances carefully he realises that he is entitled to place more money into his personal pension scheme. He consults his financial advisor about the matter and as a result tops up his pension with a lump sum of £4,000 before investing the rest as he had originally planned. Now he is confident that his pension is working as effectively as possible and that his money is invested in a more tax-efficient manner.

Before making any new investment decisions, look at your tax situation carefully and see if there are any investment vehicles which might be useful in helping your money to work harder.

Strategy #3
Be Aware of the Market

An investor who concentrates on bonds and gilts to the exclusion of all else may well find himself in a situation where he is not making the best use of his money. Being aware of the whole of the financial market and economic developments in general will help the investor to make better decisions.

You will be able to form opinions about the prospect of rising or falling interest rates, be more aware of where inflation is heading and adjust your investments accordingly. An investor who is aware of the market will also be among the first to take action when new issues are launched, if these will help you to reach your financial goals.

Example

Having read a newspaper article about the importance of financial awareness, Mr Sanders soon discovers that interest rates are said to be likely to fall over the next twelve months. Not being adverse to making the odd speculative investment, he invests £3,000 in dated gilts at par. Within seven months it is announced that interest rates are indeed to be trimmed, and as a result Mr Sanders has managed to lock himself into a position where some of his capital is earning more than it could in most other places.

Strategy #4
Evaluate Your Holdings

You should evaluate your bond- and gilt-holdings on a regular basis and make sure that your investments are on track to help you meet your objectives. Investors who are willing to take a more speculate approach to their bonds and gilts may consider selling holdings which are currently at a premium and re-invest the generated capital in other securities which are near or below par. Obviously the more often an investor evaluates his holdings, the greater the number of opportunities he will have to take such action.

Example

Mrs Dawson has been investing in bonds and gilts for many years but has only just decided to sit down and evaluate her holdings. Before long she realises that some of her gilt-holdings are currently valued at a premium, and that if she sells these she will be able to take advantage of her rising risk threshold by purchasing some new blue-chip corporate bonds.

She consults an independent financial advisor who helps her to clarify her objectives and take advantage of the holdings which are at premium. Mrs Dawson realises an immediate profit and invests in some newly issued corporate bonds at par. This now gives her the assurance of a greater level of overall profit potential as long as she holds her bonds until they mature in five years time.

Strategy #5
Compound Your Profits

Compounding profits is an excellent way to generate long term growth. If £10,000 were invested at par in a five year security with a coupon of 9%, the initial investment should produce interest of £4,500 over the whole term. If this £4,500 is reinvested, along with the original £10,000 principal, in a subsequent five-year 9% security then this new investment will generate a further £6,525 over the next half-decade. The end result is a total profit of £11,025, or 110.25% of the initial sum of capital over a period of ten years.

Of course, this is a highly simplistic example of how compounding profits can help the investor because it doesn't take into account any erosion caused by inflation. Neither does it show how re-investing interest every six months can further boost the fund. The principle of compounding, however, is clearly illustrated, and will be particularly useful to investors who are using portfolios geared for growth rather than income.

Example

Miss Grant invests £20,000 for five years in a variety of holdings and this generates an overall profit of £8,000. She doesn't really need to spend this interest income so she decides to take this £8,000 profit and reinvest it – along with the original principal of £20,000 in a similarly spread five year portfolio. If this generates a similar return then in five years she can look forward to making another £11,200 profit. Thanks to the magic of compound interest she will therefore receive a total of £39,200, having invested just £20,000 a decade earlier.

Strategy #6
Record Your Progress

If an investor is to take total control over his bond and gilt investments and stand a chance of generating professional sized profits, he must develop a habit of keeping strict records. Because bonds and gilts have lifetimes which often extend to five years and beyond, trying to recall specific details of a particular trade can be a nightmare unless organised records are kept.

Keep records of everything which is remotely related to your investments. This will include yield calculations, redemption dates, coupon yields, discount and premium figures. Having all of these details on hand will enable the investor to access the information he requires quickly and effectively without having to wade through individual security documents.

Example

Mr Travis has decided to take advantage of modern technology and computerise his finances. He obtains a suitable personal computer and appropriate software (see Chapter Nine). All that remains now is for him to enter the details of his investment into his computer system. Fortunately, Mr Travis started keeping paper records of his investments many years ago, and so all the information he needs is already available in one place – his investments file. Thanks to following the strategy of keeping strict records, the task of setting up a personal computer system takes just a few hours. Had he not kept such records, the task may well have taken several days.

Strategy #7
Review Your Performance
and Objectives

At least once each year you should set aside some time to review your performance and objectives and look ahead to the next twelve months. How have your investments performed? How has the economic situation changed? Are interest rates likely to rise or fall? How has inflation changed? How have your original objectives changed, if at all?

Asking yourself questions like these will help you make sure that your investments are as relevant now as they were the last time you reviewed them.

Example

Mr Mitchell's portfolio was designed with early retirement in mind and has generated an overall profit of 6% over the last year. This has given him a lot of confidence in his investment abilities. When he began investing he wanted to take hardly any risks, and therefore invested exclusively in dated gilts. Now he is feeling slightly more adventurous and therefore decides to begin including a few secured corporate bonds in his portfolio.

Later, Mr Mitchell decides not to take early retirement after all. He reviews his portfolio again and aims to include an even wider variety of holdings to shift the emphasis onto capital growth.

Ten years later, Mr Mitchell finally retires. Because he has developed the habit of reviewing his objectives and the performance of his portfolio, he has made a number of changes which have ensured that he can look forward to the happy retirement he has planned for so long.

Strategy #8
Don't Be Afraid to Make a Change

All investors make occasional mistakes – even professional fund managers. If a certain investment or set of investments fails to perform according to your expectations, don't be afraid to make a change if the current market values are near par or above par. In the same way, be prepared to move your money from time to time if better and more suitable investment opportunities arise.

The lifestyle of any investor will naturally change over time. Your expectations and objectives may change, as perhaps will your level of risk tolerance. Adjust your investments to suit these changes and you can be assured that your use of bonds and gilts will always be relevant to your needs.

Example

Mr Jones had security in mind when he took his first steps into the world of bond and gilt investment. Now, however, he has been fortunate enough to receive an unexpected windfall. Safety is no longer of prime concern, and so he decides to move half of his holdings into blue chip corporate bonds to help him generate more capital growth. This new portfolio has therefore changed so that it remains relevant to his improved financial status.

Summary

Advanced investment strategies are simply more involved courses of action which are designed to help the investor to either increase profits or minimise losses

✔ Strategy #1 – Sit down and review your current financial situation and future goals in a logical manner with a view to developing a solid plan of action.

✔ Strategy #2 – Don't give money away to the Inland Revenue. Make use of all tax exemptions which are available to you.

✔ Strategy #3 – Be aware of the whole of the financial market and economic developments in general. This will help you to make better investment decisions.

✔ Strategy #4 – Evaluate your bond- and gilt-holdings on a regular basis and make sure that your investments are on track to help you meet your objectives.

✔ Strategy #5 – Compound Your Profits if you are aiming for growth rather than income.

✔ Strategy #6 – Keep records of everything which is remotely related to your investments.

✔ Strategy #7 – Review your objectives and the performance of your investments at least once each year.

✔ Strategy #8 – Don't be afraid to move your money around from time to time if better and more suitable investment opportunities arise.

Chapter Eight

Bonds and Gilts in The City

F OR THE MOST part we have looked at Bonds and Gilts from the private investor's point of view. In this chapter we will take a brief look at how bonds and gilts are used by institutional investors such as professional unit trust and pension fund managers. Let us begin by examining the aims, objectives and motivations of such investors...

All institutional investors are judged by the results they generate. Their employers hire and fire on the basis of portfolio or fund performance, and this naturally puts the investor under a certain amount of pressure. He knows that there are thousands of other investors in the market-place who could replace him at a moments notice, and so his prime motivation is to make sure that the money in his care performs as well as possible – for his own sake as well as that of his employer.

This competitively charged atmosphere has led some professional investors to take what can only be described as unnecessary risks by opening large positions in highly speculative derivatives markets and the like. This, however, is often the road to ruin. What the wise investment manager must do is try to generate good profits without leaving himself vulnerable to catastrophic risks.

The key to a professional investor's success is therefore balance. Just as the private investor stands more chance of making money if he creates a balanced portfolio according to The Pyramid Principle, so the professional investor is more likely to succeed over the long term if he balances higher risk equities with more stable bonds and gilts.

The City uses a number of techniques to help them determine the optimum level of balance in a fund or portfolio. Let us take a brief look at the major techniques used...

Convertible Analysis

Because convertible bonds can be converted into actual equity holdings, they can, in some circumstances, be better than the equity itself as an investment proposition. Normally convertibles are most useful when they are undervalued, since these can give the investor a similar level of profit potential as the stock itself but generally give lower potential losses. To help them decide whether to invest in a convertible bond rather than in the underlying equity itself, convertibles are analysed using two simple mathematical calculations to provide the 'conversion' value and the 'parity' value.

Conversion value

This is how much a bond would be worth if converted to the corresponding equity. If a £1,000 convertible bond can be converted to 100 shares then the conversion value at any given moment is the number of shares available on conversion multiplied by the current share price. If the share price in this example was £10 then the conversion value would be:

$$100 \times 10 = £1,000$$

If the stock was to rise by 25%, making each share worth £12.50, then the conversion value would also increase, as follows:

$$100 \times 12.5 = £1,250$$

Similarly, if the stock was to fall by 25%, making each share worth £7.50, the conversion value would also fall, as follows:

$$100 \times 7.5 = £7.50$$

The relation between the stock price and conversion value can be seen in the illustration below:

Parity Value

Parity is the term given to a situation in which the bond and the stock underlying it have the same market value. The Parity Value of a convertible bond helps the investor to decide whether or not conversion to the stock itself would be a sensible move. The formula for parity is as follows:

$$(p/c) = (m/s)$$

Where **p** is the par value of the bond, **c** is the conversion price, **m** is the market value of the bond and **s** is the market value of the stock.

For example, if a convertible bond has a par value of £500, is convertible at £10 a share and the market value of the stock is currently £12, our formula would look like this:

$$(500/10) = (x/12)$$

The **x** in the formula is the parity figure we are looking for. We can solve the equation by simplifying the first part (500/10 = 50) and rewriting it as follows:

$$50 = x/12$$

Therefore:

$$x = 50 \times 12$$

$$x = 600$$

This formula tells use that, if this convertible bond is to be at parity, the current market value of the bond must be £600.

By calculating the conversion and parity values of convertible bonds on a regular basis, fund managers can decide whether to keep a particular bond or opt to invest in the underlying equity.

Performance Analysis

This technique is used to answer the main question regarding any fund or portfolio: How is it performing? A basic method of general performance analysis is simply to see if the portfolio is going up or down. This is often done by charting the portfolio value in order to identify a long term trend. Consider the following illustration:

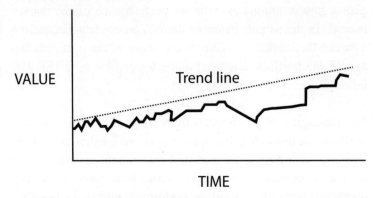

Here we can see that although the portfolio is quite volatile, the underlying trend is positive. However, this simple method of analysis is of little use on its own.

To give a more accurate idea of how well a portfolio is performing, it needs to be compared with some other economical indicator, such as the FTSE 100. This could be done by superimposing the FTSE 100 onto the original chart, as follows:

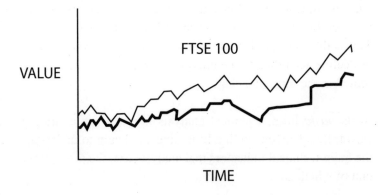

By superimposing the performance of the fund or portfolio with a standard economic indicator, the investor can see at a glance how it compares with the performance of the market overall. In this simple example there is an obvious correlation between the market movements and those of the portfolio, but overall the portfolio has been outperformed by the FTSE 100 Index.

The manager can go one step further and subject the fund or portfolio to more detailed analysis. He will often do this by charting each individual portfolio investment so that he can see which are most successful. Knowing how particular invest-ments in a portfolio or fund are performing allows the manager to gain a fairly high level of control over the final outcome by increasing successful holdings and decreasing or even elimi-nating those which are seen to be reducing the overall profits which are generated.

Technical Analysis

The decision about whether to increase fixed income investments or to focus more on equity-based investments in a fund or portfolio is often based on 'technical analysis'. This is the art of predicting whether a financial market will rise or decline according to the interpretation of historical data pre-sented in the form of a chart.

In its *basic* form, technical analysis is really quite straight-forward, and anyone with a little time can begin to understand the main technical indicators that analysts use, the most impor-tant of which are...

The Moving Average

Almost all financial institutions use the moving average. It works by charting a sample of previous market data and then superimposing a moving average which is the sum of previous data divided by the number of days used in the sample. The idea is that when the two resulting charted lines cross, an indication is given as to whether the market is more likely to rise or decline. A moving average chart usually looks something like this:

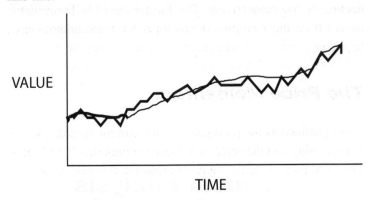

In brief, technical analysts believe that if the data line crosses the moving average line in an upward direction the market will rise. If the data line crosses the moving average line in a downward direction the market may fall.

The Moving Average Convergence / Divergence

Often abbreviated as the MACD, the Moving Average Convergence / Divergence technical indicator was developed by Gerald Appel. It is a widely used oscillator created from the divergence between two separate exponential moving averages – one calculated for the short term and another for the longer term.

When the underlying market is trending in one direction or the other, the shorter exponential moving average will rise or decline more rapidly than the longer term one. The difference between the two exponential averages is calculated and plotted on a graph as the oscillator line. As this line dips or rises above a control "zero line" so it is thought that the market may decline or rise respectively. The further the MACD oscillator moves from the zero line, the stronger the trend is thought to be.

The Price Momentum

This is defined as the ratio between the current market price of a commodity and the price of the same commodity X days ago. The formula for calculating price momentum is very simple:

$$(Current\ value - value\ X\ days\ ago) \times 100$$

If the momentum readings are high then this implies that the commodity is overbought and that a fall may be expected. If the momentum readings are low then this implies that the commodity is oversold and that a rise may be expected.

The Stochastic Indicator

This was developed by George Lane and is intended to measure – as a percentage – the position of a closing price in relation to the trading range of a previous time sample. Stochastics are thought be useful because they work on the premise that the closing price of a commodity is usually closer to the top of the trading range during a rising trend, but closer to the bottom of the trading range during a declining trend.

By oscillating between a range of 0 and 100, the stochastic is thought to indicate the way the trend is moving. A stochastic reading at or below 30 might suggest that a market rise is due, whilst a reading at or above 70 might suggest a market fall.

The Relative Strength Indicator

The Relative Strength Indicator – also known as the RSI – is a technical indicator which is believed to reveal whether a market is overbought or oversold at any particular moment in time. Basically it is an indicator which oscillates between a band of 0 and 100. If a market is overbought then this may indicate that there are too many investors holding shares.

This suggests that a fall in market value will occur when some investors dump their stock in order to take profits. If a market is oversold then this may indicate that there are too few investors holding shares. This suggests that some people will purchase shares and that the market will rise.

Mathematically speaking, the RSI is based on the ratio between previous price increases over previous price decreases, and can be expressed as follows:

$$RSI = 100 - \left(\frac{100}{\sum (+ \text{ changes} / - \text{ changes}) +1} \right)$$

Generally speaking, technical analysts work to the principle that if the RSI is above 70 then the market is overbought and a fall can be expected. Similarly, if the RSI is below 30 then the market is thought to be oversold and this may indicate a rise.

Volume Accumulation Indicator

This technical indicator was created by Marc Chaikin. It measures trading volume in relation to price fluctuations, working on the hypothesis that if a market spends most of the day on a downward trend, but ends on a positive note, the positive trend should be interpreted in relation to the whole, which was largely negative.

The Volume Accumulation Formula looks like this:

$$VA = (((MC\text{-}ML)\text{-}(MH\text{-}MC)) / (MH\text{-}ML)) \times V$$

Where **VA** is Volume Accumulation, **MC** is the Market Close, **ML** is the Market Low, **MH** is the Market High and **V** is the Volume.

This indicator is interpreted by comparing it with the market price and the appearance of prominent convergences and divergences are said to indicate likely changes in the market trend.

All of these technical analysis indicators are used to indicate possible increases or declines in the underlying market on which they are based.

Most are generated automatically by computers which are linked up to live data feeds. This gives financial institutions a highly accurate idea of how the markets are trending at any given moment. (The next chapter will discuss how you can use a personal computer to get a similar picture of the markets using technical analysis indicators).

If a fund manager takes the broad market as a whole and is of the opinion that it is about to enjoy a bullish phase then he may decide that focusing on equity based investments may be better than focusing on fixed income securities. If, on the other hand, he believes that the market is about to go through a bearish period then he may wish to avoid taking out more equity investments and concentrate on creating known stability with more bonds and gilts.

Risk Analysis

Because fund managers and the like do not want to wait until (say) interest rates have actually risen before they know how their investment will react in that situation, they often create 'analysis models'.

These allow them to hypothesise about what might conceivably take place in the future and plan what they would do if these events actually happened. By doing this they will immediately know what to do should an interest rate rise be announced. All of this helps to make the fund or portfolio as adaptable to change as possible.

Before hypothetical analysis models can be created a benchmark or base model must be drawn up. This would be a graphical and statistical representation of how the fund can be expected to perform if the current economical factors remain fairly stable throughout the term of the investments. Such a base model would take into account the known fixed income which bonds and gilts generate and it would also aim to create an accurate projection of how much profit equity investments might bring. A base model might look something like this:

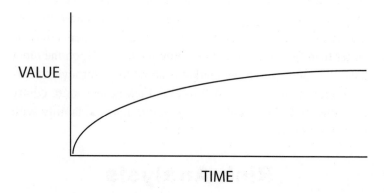

Advanced computer technology allows the managers to create almost any financial scenario and see how their investments would fare in comparison with a base model such as this. By entering a variety of statistical data representing interest rates, currency fluctuations and the like, the manager will be able to highlight any fund weaknesses which become apparent.

Three analysis techniques which are often applied using computer models are known as the Shift, Twist and Butterfly. These are complex mathematical formulae which can be expressed graphically and are said to fit most types of portfolio or fund fluctuations.

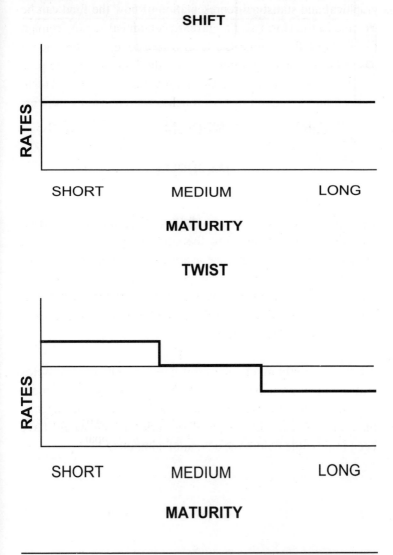

SHIFT

MATURITY

TWIST

MATURITY

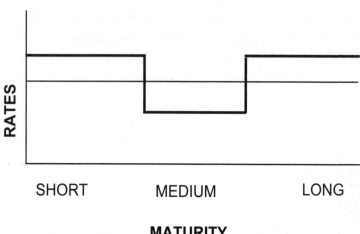

BUTTERFLY

By applying the Shift, Twist and Butterfly standard deviations (and their mirror images) to the underlying data of the base model, the manager can once again get a clearer view of how the money he is investing may perform. If it is on target then the fund can be maintained as it is. If these analysis techniques do highlight any flaws then these can be looked at in greater detail and amended accordingly.

There is no room in a book of this type to explain the complex mathematical principles which lie behind these analysis models, but suffice it to say that they enable the fund manager to plan ahead for a wide range of scenarios which would have been impossible before the advent of computers.

Duration Analysis

Duration analysis is something which is very important where fixed income securities are concerned. It was built on the contents of a paper published in 1938 by F. Macaulay. Hence the formula used is sometimes referred to as the Macaulay Duration Formula.

To define the "Macaulay Duration Formula" simply, it gives the investor a figure which can be interpreted as the weighted average of the amount of time it takes for the cash generated by fixed income securities to reach the investor. The formula itself looks like this:

$$\text{Duration} = \frac{\sum (A(\text{Cash})_t \times t)}{C}$$

Where **A(Cash)** is the current value of the cash to be received at a stated time **t** (this is figured using a rate equal to the fixed security's Yield to Maturity figure) and **C** represents the current market value of the security.

The duration figure generated by the use of this formula is used in a number of ways by institutional investors. Most commonly, it is used to:

◆ Help the investor create a balanced portfolio which needs to be sure of meeting a set target.

◆ Help the investor correctly hedge a portfolio of fixed income investments.

◆ Help the investor compare one fixed income security with another and highlight the sensitivity of each to possible changes in interest rates.

All of these types of analysis are used by City institutions for one purpose, and one purpose only: to develop and maintain a balance of risk and reward in a fund or portfolio which is reliable enough to meet known goals (such as to pay for the pensions of company employees) and is at the same time flexible enough to adapt to any future economic changes.

Bonds and gilts are the tools which professional investors use to balance their equity investments so that this two-fold aim of fund reliability and flexibility is reached.

Summary

✔ Bonds and Gilts are just as important to institutional investors as they are to private individuals.

✔ The aim of institutional investors is to generate good fund performance without exposing the money they control to unnecessarily high risks. They achieve this by maintaining a sense of balance in the fund, using bonds and gilts to provide fixed income and stability and investing in equity to generate good returns.

✔ The City uses a number of methods to analyse their investments, the market and previous performance. They also use analysis techniques to show them how their investments might fare in a number of economic environments by using mathematical models based on hypothetical interest rate increases, etc.

✔ To fully understand how institutional investors control risk and reward to maintain a balanced portfolio of investments, you should study the topic in further detail.

Chapter Nine

Computer Aided Investment

We have touched upon a lot of technical information in the eight previous chapters, and you may well be wondering how on earth anyone could ever have the time to keep track of bond and gilt prices, premiums, discounts, calculate yields *and* maintain proper financial records. After all, most of us have day jobs, don't we? Or at least other commitments which we must attend to. Does this mean that hands-on financial investment is reserved only for those who have nothing else to do?

Maybe a few decades ago such a conclusion would have been accurate. Back then, private investors had to do things the hard way – with a pad and pencil – and the only help they had was the humble pocket calculator. These days however, things are different. The personal computer has brought active private investment within the reach of anyone who truly wants to get involved.

Although many private investors are sceptical about relying on technology to help them take care of their money, a personal computer, or PC, can be the best friend you will ever have in the world of finance. Not only can it perform pages of advanced mathematical calculations within a fraction of a second, it can also help you to keep track of your investments with pinpoint accuracy and even suggest which way the stockmarket could be heading thanks to automated technical analysis capabilities. In short, a modern personal computer can be likened to a personal financial assistant who is on call twenty-four hours a day, seven days a week, to provide you will all the up-to-the-minute information you need to succeed as a private investor.

In this chapter we will look at all aspects of computer aided investing, from the hardware and software most commonly used through to a discussion of data feeds and on-line trading (for those of you who also invest in company shares). Let us begin then, by first of all talking about...

The Personal Computer

A modern personal computer can be divided into six separate components for the purposes of discussion. These are:

Central Processing Unit (CPU)

The CPU is the "brain" of a personal computer, since it is responsible for processing all of the information it receives. The effectiveness of the CPU is generally gauged by the speed at which it operates, measured in Hertz (Hz), Megahertz (Mhz) and Gigahertz (Ghz). A computer which operates at 3.0Ghz (Gigahertz) will therefore be a lot more effective than one that operates at 2.0Ghz.

Random Access Memory (RAM)

The RAM is the "short-term memory" of a personal computer. The more RAM a computer has, the more easily and efficiently it will be able to deal with the information it manages. RAM is measured in Kilobytes (K), Megabytes (MB) and Gigabytes (GB). For the record, one kilobyte of memory can hold 1,024 bits of information, one megabyte is equal to 1,000K and one Gigabyte is equal to 1,000MB.

When personal computers were first introduced to the general public, Bill Gates, founder of Microsoft, commented that "640K of memory should be enough for anyone." Whilst this may have been true at the time, computer technology has advanced rapidly since the early days and today you won't find many machines for sale with less than several GB of RAM as standard. Indeed, the amount of RAM that personal computers boast increases from year to year, so the rule of thumb here is to choose a machine that as much RAM you can afford.

The Hard Disk

The hard disk is where the computer can permanently store information for future reference. Again, the larger the hard disk in terms of capacity, the better it is for the user. Hard disk capacity, like Random Access Memory, is measured in megabytes and gigabytes.

Optical Disk Drive

An optical disc drive allows the computer to read and/or write information from and to optical media such as Compacts Discs

(CDs) and Digital Versatile Discs (DVDs). The efficiency of an optical disc drive is gauged by its speed. The faster an optical drive can read and write information from and to the media, the better.

The Monitor

The monitor is a visual display unit that presents images generated by the computer. Computer monitors have evolved at roughly the same rate as television screens, and so a modern monitor uses flat screen LCD technology as opposed to an old-fashioned cathode ray tube (CRT). This enables monitors to provide a large display without taking up an unacceptable amount of desk space. As far as the private investor is concerned, a huge display is generally unnecessary, so a fairly standard 19" screen is perfectly acceptable.

Internet Capability

Having some kind of internet access is almost essential in the modern world, and buying a personal computer that is not 'internet-ready' is usually a false economy. The type of internet access you can get will depend to a great extent on your geographical location. Most people can be connected to the internet via a cable or broadband service, but in some cases a service that uses satellite technology might need to be employed instead. Whatever methods of internet access you have to choose from, you should opt for the fastest service possible. This will generally be the one with the highest bandwidth, measured in megabits per second (Mbps). A service offering 50Mbps would therefore be better than one offering 10Mbps.

Now, although the actual components themselves (CPU,

RAM, hard disk, optical disc drive and monitor) will probably remain much the same for the foreseeable future, all of the above information is subject to change as technology continues to improve. You should therefore expect personal computers to become even faster and more efficient as the years roll by.

The rule of thumb to use when buying a personal computer is therefore to buy as much power you can afford – but don't let numbers go to your head. Just because a new machine with a faster CPU and more RAM becomes available doesn't mean that your old one is now defunct. The fact is that a good PC can serve you well long after it has gone out of "style".

Software

Once you have a computer, you will need some software. This comes in all shapes and sizes and is readily available through PC magazines or from computer stores, but before you rush out to buy a software title, you first need to spend some time thinking carefully about how you want your computer to help you as a private investor. Here are just some of the ways in which your PC can help you. Select whatever options seem most appropriate to you and then make sure that any software you purchase can meet your needs in full. This will prevent you from buying a costly product which you may never fully benefit from.

General Financial Organisation

This is simply the organisation and tracking of your personal or small business finances. You begin by telling your PC how much you have in your bank accounts, or on your credit cards, and then every time you spend or receive money, you record the transaction on the computer. Your PC then updates all of your balances accordingly so that you always know what your bottom line is.

This is the most basic way in which your PC can help you with your finances, and the need is catered for by packages such as *Microsoft Money* and Intuit's *Quicken*.

Share Price Tracking

If you invest in shares as well as in bonds and gilts then you may be interested in using your computer to perform share price tracking. This is where your PC takes share prices and records them for future reference. The data can be shown in the form of a stock chart and some packages will also enable you to use some simple technical analysis tools such as moving averages, stochastics and so on.

Almost any spreadsheet (such as Microsoft's Excel) will help you to keep track of your shares, so if you already have such a package and all you want is to track a handful of stock market prices, you may well find that you already have all you need as far as this is concerned.

Internet Data Retrieval

Internet data retrieval is a method of obtaining financial market data from an online source and downloading it to your own computer. All you need to enjoy the benefits of internet data retrieval is a computer with internet access and a reliable source of information about the financial markets you are interested in.

Assuming that your computer already has internet access (if it doesn't you will need to arrange this) you can find reliable information sources by visiting an internet search engine (for example, www.google.com) and performing a search on a few key words that summarise the information you need.

For example, you could search for "FTSE 100 data download" or "NASDAQ data download" and the search engine would highlight the internet sites that are most relevant. From there, all you have to do is browse the sites and make up your own mind as to which source of data would best suit your needs.

The most reliable data on the internet is not, in my opinion, free. The most reliable companies which allow you to download their information charge a small monthly or annual fee for the privilege. Of course, how much you are prepared to pay depends on how valuable the information is to you and how valuable your time is, but don't expect a totally free ride as far as reliable data is concerned.

Intra-Day Data Retrieval

If downloading data once a day or once a week is no good to you – perhaps because you want to track intra-day price movements – another option is to purchase a software package which will enable you to download data several times a day almost automatically.

These software packages use your internet connection to download the relevant data from specific sources. Usually, but not always, the sources used are associated with the publisher of the intra-day software itself.

Intra-Day retrieval is almost always the most expensive way of downloading data via the internet because the source company which allows you to download will charge you according to how often you access their information. That said, if you invest in bonds and gilts frequently and use intra-day data to generate good profits, this additional expense may well be off-set by even greater profits.

Technical Analysis

Because computers can process masses of mathematical information in a matter of second, they are ideal for the application of technical analysis tools. At the click of a button, your PC can produce moving averages, relative strength indicators, over-bought and over-sold signals and much, much more.

If you would like to get involved in performing technical analysis on company shares (perhaps as a way of deciding whether to exercise the conversion option on convertible bonds) this facility will save you a lot of time in calculating moving averages, etc., using just a calculator. Even better, because personal computers are dab-hands at math, you can virtually guarantee that any technical analysis indicators used will be accurate to the nth degree.

Spreadsheets are capable of producing technical analysis indicators as long as you know how to implement the formula itself, but if you intend to use technical analysis on a regular basis you would be better served by investing in a stand-alone package which is designed specifically for this purpose.

Automatic Signal Generation

Finally, your PC has the power to do the ultimate as far as stock market prediction is concerned: it can automatically retrieve and analyse market data, then signal you every time it comes across what it considers to be a new direction in the market as whole, or when it comes across what it considers to be "buy" and "sell" signals for specific company shares..

To enjoy the luxury of such automation, you will need to invest in a whistles-and-bells software package which can routinely download information from the internet and perform technical analysis on your behalf. These can be expensive, but if you are serious about becoming a successful private investor then the expense involved in acquiring such software will be more than justified by the time you save and the signals it generates.

Of course, you don't have to act every time the computer finds a buy or sell signal, but it's good to know that you won't miss a trading opportunity just because you didn't have time to manually look at every chart for every stock you track on your PC.

On-Line Investing

As well as helping you to retrieve, analyse and interpret a wide variety of market data, your PC can also help you when it comes to actually buying and selling shares in particular. How? By giving you access to on-line stock market brokers.

Of course, to trade over the internet you will need an internet connection and an account with a suitable on-line broker (such as Charles Schwab Online) but once those preliminaries have been arranged, your PC will provide you with true freedom as far as investing is concerned. You will be able to place buy or sell orders twenty-four hours a day, seven days a week, ensuring that your instructions are carried out just as soon as the market allows. You will be able to check up on the state of your investment at the push of a button. Use internet trading in conjunction with internet banking and it is no exaggeration to say that your humble PC can begin to play a central part in the organisation and use of your finances.

With on-line trading there is no waiting for your broker to pick up his telephone. There is no waiting to issue instructions on a busy Monday morning. At last, all private investors have the opportunity to take immediate investment action and reap the rewards. These are just some of the reasons why on-line investing has become the number one method of buying and selling bonds and gilts in the 21st century. Telephone calls and personal visits to brokers can still be useful, of course, but on-line investing is generally a lot more convenient as far as day to day transactions are concerned.

As you begin to look at how you want your computer to help you invest more successfully in shares, you may well find that you have a need we have not discussed here. If so, don't worry. There are many different software packages available and many more being developed, so the chances of you finding one which almost exactly meets your needs are exceptional.

Mobile Computing

Having discussed the use of personal computers, let us briefly turn our attention to an even more convenient way of investing, and that is by taking full advantage of today's mobile computing solutions.

Mobile computers are – quite simply – laptop, notebook or palmtop computers which are fully portable. They can be transported in a briefcase or even in your pocket, and used "on the move". Even better from a private investors point of view, most modern portable computers can access the internet using WiFi or mobile phone technology.

The benefit of this is that even if you are sitting by the pool on your vacation, you can still download your usual financial data, have the computer analyse the information and then, if you decide that it is time to act, use your mobile to place a buy or sell order with your broker. Thus, you have a great opportunity to generate investment profits without sacrificing any of your tanning hours.

Mobile computers are often smaller version of their desktop predecessors. Like any normal PCs, mobile computers have central processing units, random access memory, display units (usually liquid crystal displays built into the computer itself) and a facility for storing information permanently on a hard disk. Whilst it used to be true that a mobile computer had far fewer "bells and whistles" than a desktop model, technology in this area has progressed so fast that this is simply no longer the case. If you have the cash to invest you can bet your bottom dollar that there is a mobile computer out there which will put your normal PC to shame.

If you don't think that mobile computing is something you need right now then you are probably right, but don't write the whole subject off just yet. If you begin using a normal desktop personal computer to help you make your financial investment decisions and this proves to be successful, it won't be long before you start thinking seriously about investing whilst on the move.

Summary

✔ Personal computers can **help** the private investor in many ways. They can crunch numbers, record your investments and – thanks to technical analysis – even suggest which way the stock market as a whole might be heading.

✔ Personal computers can be divided into six major components: the Central Processing Unit (CPU), Random Access Memory (RAM), hard disk, optical disc drive, monitor and internet capability.

✔ To get the most out of a personal computer, you need to buy **software** which is most suited to your needs. There is a wide range of PC software for the private investor to choose from, so know what you want from a package before you buy.

✔ **Mobile computing** is becoming increasingly popular, and the bonds and gilts investor can use laptop, notebook and palmtop computers to help them monitor their investments and make new ones even when they do not have access to their usual desktop PC.

✔ A personal computer will not make you an automatic financial whiz, but it can be an **invaluable aid** for the serious investor when used in conjunction with your own knowledge and common sense.

Glossary

At Discount
The term used to describe a situation in which the current market value of a bond or gilt is less than the par value.

At Par
The term used to describe a situation in which the current market value of a bond or gilt is equal to the par value.

At Premium
The term used to describe a situation in which the current market value of a bond or gilt is greater than the par value.

Bond
A promise from a company to pay a lender of money a fixed sum of interest on a regular basis for a stated period. At the end of this period the original loan, or principal, is paid.

Bond-holder
A person who has invested in a bond or bonds.

Capital Gain
The profit realised on an investment or asset when it is sold.

Capital Loss
A loss realised on an investment or asset when it is sold.

Corporate Bond
Also known as Loan Stocks, corporate bonds are bonds which are issued by companies for the purpose of raising finance.

Convertible Bond
A corporate bond which gives the holder the option – but not the obligation – to convert his holding into ordinary shares at a fixed price.

Coupon Yield
Also known as Nominal Yield, this is the amount of interest – usually expressed as a percentage – which an investor will receive each year on his bond or gilt.

Cum-Dividend
A security or share which allows the investor to receive all of the interest which has accrued since the last official dividend payment date.

Current Market Value
This is the amount for which a bond or gilt can be purchased or sold in the current market conditions. As market demand rises, so will the current market value, and vice versa.

Default
The term used to describe a situation where a bond or gilt issuer fails to meet his financial obligations to the bond or gilt investor.

Ex-Dividend
A security or share which does not allow the investor to receive any interest which is due on the next official dividend payment date.

Euro-Bond
Bonds issued in a currency other than that of the country in which the bond issuer is based.

Face Value
See **Par Value**.

Gilt-holder
A person who has invested in a gilt or gilts.

Guaranteed Income Bond
A fixed rate bond usually issued by an insurance company and which cannot be traded on the market during its lifetime.

Inflation
A reduction in the purchasing power of money due to a sustained increase in the Retail Price Index.

Issue Date
The date on which a bond or gilt is issued.

Junk Bond
A very high risk bond that offers substantially higher returns but is very risky.

Liquidity
The ease with which money tied up in an investment can be realised. If an investment can be sold quickly then it is said to have high liquidity.

Loan Stock
See **Corporate Bond**.

Longs
A long-term bond or gilt which matures in more than fifteen years.

Maturity
The term given to the end of the lifespan of a bond or gilt.

Mediums
A medium-term bond or gilt which matures in anything between five and fifteen years time.

Nominal Yield
See **Coupon Yield**.

Par Value
Also known as Face Value. This is the cost of a bond or gilt on issue and the amount of money which the investor will receive on the redemption date.

Principal
The original amount of capital borrowed by a bond or gilt issuer or lent by an investor.

Redemption Value
The value for which a bond or gilt may be redeemed when it matures.

Retail Price Index
A mathematical index which is used to measure changes in the cost of living. Commonly referred to as the RPI.

Secured Bond
A corporate bond which is backed by specific company assets.

Shorts
A short-term bond or gilt which matures in less than five years.

Unsecured Bond
A corporate bond which is not backed by specific company assets.

Yield
The amount of interest or profit which an investment generates over a given period.

Zero Bond
A corporate bond which does not pay interest annually. Zero bonds are issued at deep discount from their redemption value and appreciate gradually as they reach maturity. Sometimes referred to as zero-coupon bonds.